Text by Dr. Kenneth Norris (Whales & Porpoises), Dr. Burney Le Boeuf (Pinnipeds), Dan Miller, recent head of the Sea Otter Program, State of California, and Rachel Saunders, biologist with the Friends of the Sea Otter, Carmel; illustrations by Gregory Irons, with some help with whales from Dr. Ray Gilmore.

D1560945

Here is a sea otter rushing to get a copy of DOS CALIFORNIOS, an exciting book about an old sea otter in California in 1818, printed in both English and Spanish. It is just $2.95 at your store, or write us.

Great Blue Whale *(Balaenoptera musculus)*

The great blue whale lives in all the oceans of the world and is the largest animal that ever lived on Earth. It reaches about a hundred feet in length and may weigh one hundred and thirty tons. To see one of these huge whales swimming alongside your ship is a sight never to be forgotten. Blue whales are very swift swimmers and can outdistance most ships; they can cruise over twenty knots and may go quite a lot faster when frightened. Because of their size, blue whales were a very valuable prize to whalers, and once ships became fast enough to catch the blue whale, they became the major prize in the ocean. Hundreds of thousands of them were taken by whalers during the decades from 1930 to 1950. This huge fishery for blue whales soon reduced their numbers to a very low level and people began to worry that they might become extinct; but, fortunately, the whaling for them was stopped before they were driven to extinction, and they now seem to be slowly increasing in numbers.

Blue whales make very peculiar sounds so low that humans cannot hear them. However, when one makes a recording of the blue whale's sound and then speeds it

Slate blue (almost gray-blue, with a faint mottling and faint cross-striping); the belly is almost as dark as the back, and the undersides of the flippers are milk-white.

TOSHIRO MIFUNE
TO SCALE

up, one is then able to hear it. Blue whales themselves apparently can hear these sounds for very long distances in the ocean, and may actually be using them to communicate back and forth over many miles of ocean. The blue whale is called a blue whale because of its grayish or bluish color. Typically, blue whales are mottled grayish-blue animals without a very white belly, such as that found on many marine mammals. Sometimes the bellies of blue whales become covered with a film of tiny plants, called diatoms, which turn their stomachs yellow, and this has given rise to the old name, "sulfur bottom" whale, for the blue whale.

Blue whales feed on only one kind of little shrimp, or krill, in the waters of the southern hemisphere, though in the northern hemisphere they seem to feed on several different species of similar crustaceans. Blue whales, which belong to the group of large whales called *rorquals*, are baleen whales. The baleen consists of horny plates hanging from the roof of the mouth of the whale, which form a kind of strainer. The whales feed by swimming along with their mouths open very wide in order to take in large mouthfuls of water; they then close their mouths, inflating the lower throat pouch, which is lined with grooves to allow the throat to expand, and the water is forced out through the baleen. Anything caught in that natural strainer is then licked off with the great tongue of the whale and swallowed. Other whales feed in other ways; some simply swim along, passing water through their open mouths, and some grub in the sea bottom.

Right Whale *(Eubalaena glacialis)*

Right whales live in the cold waters of both hemispheres. They are skimming whales; that is they feed by opening their mouths slightly and swim along so that water is forced inside their mouth, and then out through the very long baleen. These whales have huge, arching lower lips that cover up the baleen and dip down at the back end to the angles of the mouth where the eyes are located. Most right whales have bonnets on their heads, which are peculiar thickenings of the skin, and are sometimes infested with worms and other parasites. Right whales give birth to their calves in shallow water, near shore, in many places around the world. One of the largest populations lives in Argentina, and comes into large, quiet bays in the southern part of that country. Another large population occurs in South Africa, where the whales congregate in shallow bays along the southern shore. The spout of right whales is often slightly double, which is not surprising since these big baleen whales have two nostrils on the top of their heads instead of a single blow-hole such as the dolphins have. Actually, the big baleen whales are really very different from the dolphins and have been separate from them for probably sixty

Shiny black, sometimes with white markings on its belly.

million years or more. At least one ancestor of the baleen whales had peg-like teeth, but it is not sure whether or not it had baleen. No one knows when baleen first developed. You can imagine what it may have come from if you run your tongue over the roof of your own mouth, and feel the ridges that are there. They may have simply grown out to form this important food-getting apparatus for the whales.

California Gray Whales *(Eschrichtius robustus)*

In one lagoon in Mexico there are whales, called "friendly whales," which come up to and play with boats that ply those waters, sometimes forcing them part way out of the water and letting them slide down their mottled backs. Gray whales are mottled with grayish or whitish blotches. They carry many parasites, such as barnacles, and great patches of a crustacean called a whale louse. These whale lice live on even the youngest babies and seem to leave the mother for the newborn young at the time of birth. Like many whales, gray whales leap into the air on occasion, and perform what are called breaches; this is where a whale leaps ponderously into the air, turns on its side, and falls back into the water with a great splash. They also pitchpole, which means they place their tails on the bottom of the lagoons and force their heads up out of the water so that they stand upright in the water, sometimes with their heads reaching eight or ten feet above the surface. They then slowly fall back into the water as they tip out of balance.

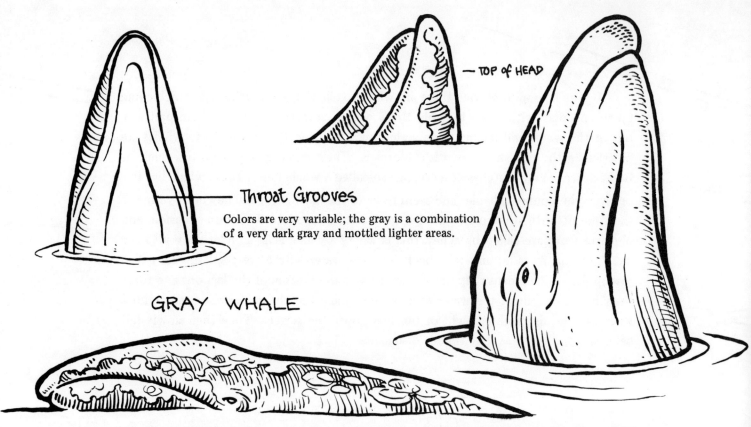

Throat Grooves

Colors are very variable; the gray is a combination of a very dark gray and mottled lighter areas.

— TOP of HEAD

GRAY WHALE

The California gray whale is a living fossil; whales almost identical to it swam in the bays of California twenty million or more years ago. At one time gray whales lived on both sides of the Atlantic and in the western Pacific, where they went into the great inland sea in southern Japan. At present they are known only in the eastern Pacific near the western coast of the United States, although a few are occasionally seen in Korea. In the waters of the Arctic Sea, the gray whale feeds on the shallow, muddy bottom of the Bering and Chukchi Seas. There they suck up crustaceans that live in burrows in the muddy bottom and eat them by the basketful.

The California gray whale makes a tremendous migration, going from near the ice edge in the Arctic Sea down into the warm waters of Mexico, where the mothers bear their calves. The whales travel as a procession, with the pregnant females going first and reaching the lagoons, first entering them and going deep into the quiet waters in their recesses. There, the gray whales apparently give birth to the young head first and into the air. Later, the males and the non-pregnant females and young animals come south and also gather around the lagoons but do not normally go deep into them. One wonders if those lagoons are essential to the whale and, if people destroy them with boats or oil derricks, whether the gray whale will survive.

Gray whales are moderate-sized baleen whales, reaching a length of about forty-eight feet. The females of the gray whale are slightly larger than the males, and it is thought that this is because they have to nurse a baby during the long migration, for in the entire migration, which may take six months or so, they eat little or nothing, but instead live off their great blanket of blubber; so not only must the adult whale itself live off this blanket, but it must feed a hungry young whale that is growing very rapidly indeed. Gray whales give birth every other year, and then spend the year in between resting and building up their blubber coat. Gray whales are about fourteen to fifteen feet long when they are born, and by the time they leave the lagoons a month later, they may have reached twenty feet in length.

Pilot Whale *(Globicephala melaena)*

Very black and shiny, with a little white streak from the center of the chest to the abdomen; at the chest there is a heart-shaped spot of white, tapering off to long streaks.

Pilot whales are very social animals, and live in large schools in all the oceans of the world. There are tropical pilot whales, and other species that live in cold water, both off the northern coasts of North America and Europe, and in the southern hemisphere. Schools of pilot whales usually move rather slowly through the ocean, though sometimes they can be seen riding together inside the crashing waves of storms at sea. Pilot whales often dive for their food, sometimes going deep to capture prey far down in the dark ocean where light never penetrates. The fat forehead of the pilot whale contains what is called the "melon," an almost football-shaped mass of fat used by the whale to focus its sound into a beam which it can then direct in front of it as it swims along, to catch prey and avoid obstacles. Mostly they feed on small squid, which they will eat by the hundreds. When pilot whales are searching for their food they will swim in broad ranks, spread out for as much as a mile across the ocean from side to side. This broad rank of animals lets the school sweep a large area of sea with their sounds, so that they can locate prey in a large piece of ocean. Once the food is found the whales all gather around and begin to feed. Often in the afternoon the whales will form what is called a loafing group, in which they congregate in a more or less circular gathering of whales, some lying on their backs, some swimming slowly along right side up, and others poking their heads out of the water or even doing the opposite, turning over and sticking their tails up into the air. Pilot whales have been kept in captivity, and have become quite tame. Old male pilot whales, however, often stay quite fierce throughout a life in captivity, and may even kill other animals in the oceanariums, sometimes by ramming into them at high speed. Pilot whales are one of the peculiar whale species that often runs aground. The whole school may swim up onto a beach and die. No one is really sure exactly why they do this, but the most likely explanation seems to be that schools can catch epidemic diseases of various kinds, and that the whales in these stranding groups are sick.

Fin Whale (*Balaenoptera physalus*)

Here two fin whales are seen swimming dangerously near to a whaling factory ship and a catcher vessel. The fin whale was for many years the mainstay of the world fishery. It is found in all seas, but was especially abundant in the Antarctic and the north Atlantic and north Pacific Oceans. The finback whale is a very swift-swimming species that can travel at well over twenty knots for considerable periods

Dark color, but not glistening, with milk-white shiny belly up to and almost beyond the dorsal fin; the upper lip is whitish on the right side only

of time. Because it was so swift, it and other members of the genus, *Balaenoptera*, were not fished by the early whalers using sailing vessels; the whales were simply too fast to catch. But when steam vessels came into use, the finback became vulnerable to them, and began to be captured in large numbers.

The finback is one of the whales that makes a long migration, from polar waters where it feeds during the summer, to subtropical waters where the calves are born out in the open sea. No one knows very much about the birthing areas or about the process of birth itself for these giant animals, which may reach approximately eighty to eighty-five feet in length. The finback whale is interesting because one of its lips is white and the other is black, and so is the straining mechanism, or

Breathing - Diving Rhythm

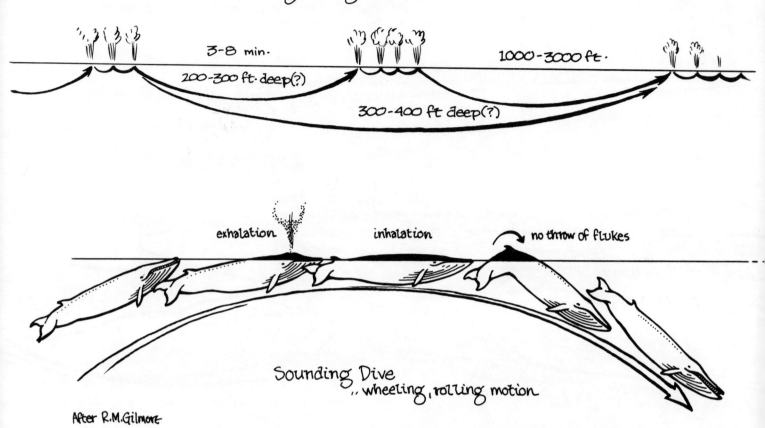

3-8 min.

200-300 ft. deep(?)

1000-3000 ft.

300-400 ft deep(?)

exhalation   inhalation   no throw of flukes

Sounding Dive
.. wheeling, rolling motion

After R.M.Gilmore

baleen, on the inside of the whale's mouth. Apparently this is because it turns on its side to feed on the tiny crustaceans, or krill, that make up its major diet. The white lips perhaps help to herd the plankton so that the animal can capture it more easily, though no one really knows.

Finback whales make a peculiar sound, which is so low that not many people can hear it. It is a sound produced at approximately twenty cycles per second, which is repeated monotonously for hours at a time by swimming finback whales. No one is exactly sure why they make these sounds, but they may communicate between each other with the signals or they may actually navigate by using them.

♂   ♀

Whales Mating

Single spout to 15 feet.

← front

Long, smooth, black back and sides. White belly, conspicuous fin 18-24 inches, on rear back.

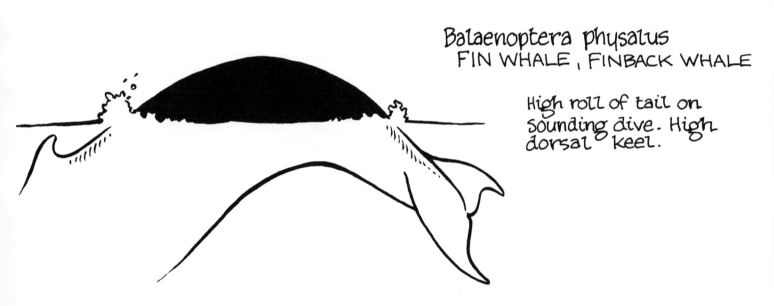

Balaenoptera physalus
FIN WHALE, FINBACK WHALE

High roll of tail on sounding dive. High dorsal keel.

Asymmetrically white on right side, upper jaw & front third of baleen. Black on left side.

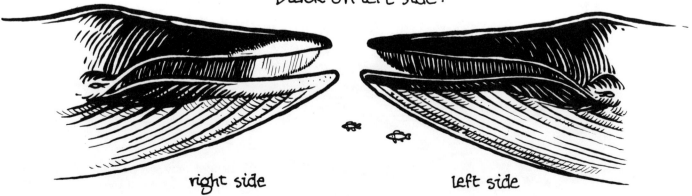

right side

left side

after R.M.

Sperm Whale *(Physeter catodon)*

Almost uniform brownish gray, but with little white patches on the chin, mouth corner

The sperm whale is one of the most peculiar animals in the world. Its body may be as much as one-third nose, that is to say the head of the animal is extremely large, and the complicated nostrils on its head may run for as much as a third of the length of the animal. It has a wrinkly, brownish skin, and hardly any dorsal fin at all, but rather a kind of irregular hump in its place. It has large paddle-shaped pectoral flippers and a huge, long, narrow jaw lined with heavy, blunt, ivory teeth. These teeth are found only on the lower jaw in most sperm whales, and fit into sockets in the gums on the upper jaw when the animal closes its mouth. Occasionally sperm whales will be found with numbers of teeth embedded in the gums of the upper jaw, but they do not seem to be good for much. Sperm whales feed very deep in the

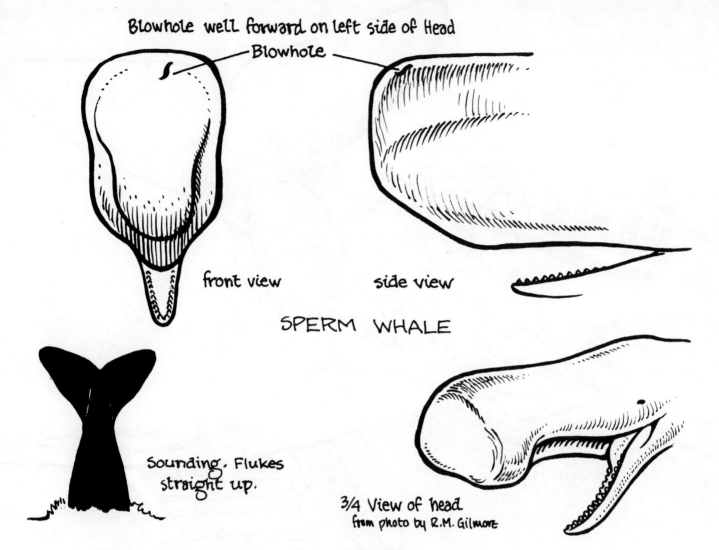

Blowhole well forward on left side of Head

Blowhole

front view

side view

SPERM WHALE

Sounding. Flukes straight up.

3/4 View of head
from photo by R.M. Gilmore

ocean and are perhaps the champion divers in the sea. They have been found entangled in submarine telephone cables down at least 3,600 feet below the surface, and other evidence suggests that they may go twice that deep or more in search of prey. The sperm whale feeds mostly on squid, some of them very large. It also eats fish it catches on the bottom, down in the dark sea where no light ever penetrates. Some people think that it drags its jaw in the mud and scares these fish up into the water where they may be caught, but no one is really sure.

Unlike other whales, the sperm whale produces a spout which is directed forward at about a forty-five-degree angle to the sea surface. The spouts of other whales go straight up in the air. When you see a whale making such a spout, even from a very long distance, you can be sure that it is a sperm whale, and as you come closer you can see that the animal has a peculiar box-like head with a front end that is straight up and down to the water. When you see the wrinkles on its back and the peculiar dorsal fin, you can be sure you have seen a sperm whale. Male sperm whales grow to be about twice as long and several times as heavy as the females of the species. They are quite fierce creatures, at least to each other, and to whalers who try to harpoon them. Fights between male sperm whales have been described in which the two whales rush at each other swimming upside down with their mouths open, and then lock their peculiar long jaws together and thrash about at the sea surface. Sometimes these fights result in the dislocation of the jaw of one of the whales. Sperm whales apparently make only one sort of sound, a crashing bang-like sound so loud that it may travel for as much as fifteen miles in the ocean. The whales use these sounds for all of the signaling that they do, and it is probable that the sounds are very complex and carry a lot of different meanings for the whale.

The sperm whale has long been a major species captured by whalers. It is used almost entirely for the oil it produces, while the meat is not often eaten. Sperm whale oil is divided into two kinds: one a very fine waxy oil that comes from the forehead of the whale inside a great structure called the case; and the more ordinary oil which is taken from the blubber of the whale. Spermaceti, from the forehead of the whale, at one time was used for the finest of candles. Sperm whales are born in warm waters not too far from the equator; mothers and calves swim northward but do not go more than about halfway to the pole in this migration, while the old males will often go much farther; sometimes they are found relatively near the ice edge.

Two Humpback Whales

Humpback Whale & Calf (*Megaptera novaeangliae*)

The humpback mother and calf in this picture are being visited by a diver. These peculiar whales bear their babies, which are born at fourteen to fifteen feet in length, in subtropical seas, in such places as Hawaii, in Tonga, in the Austral Islands near New Zealand, in some islands off Mexico, and on a series of offshore banks in the Caribbean sea. Usually the humpback whale will seek out such islands or shorelines for its calving. Like the other large whales, it feeds primarily in polar latitudes, though it does eat some food along the migration path. Humpback whales sing peculiar calls, or songs, as much as nine minutes in length, and composed of a bewildering combination of mews, groans, and other sounds, in a series which is repeated over and over, on the calving and breeding grounds. These songs seem to stay relatively constant throughout a given season on the calving grounds, and even the next year one seems to be able to recognize the same songs being sung by the whales though they do change a little from year to year.

Humpback whales seem to fly underwater with their great, long pectoral fins stuck out to the side like the wings of jet planes. They fly along with great ponderous beats of their huge flukes, and may gain enough speed so that they can actually leap completely free of the water. Sometimes when they are mating, whales will jump free of the water, clasping one another with these long, strap-like flippers. The

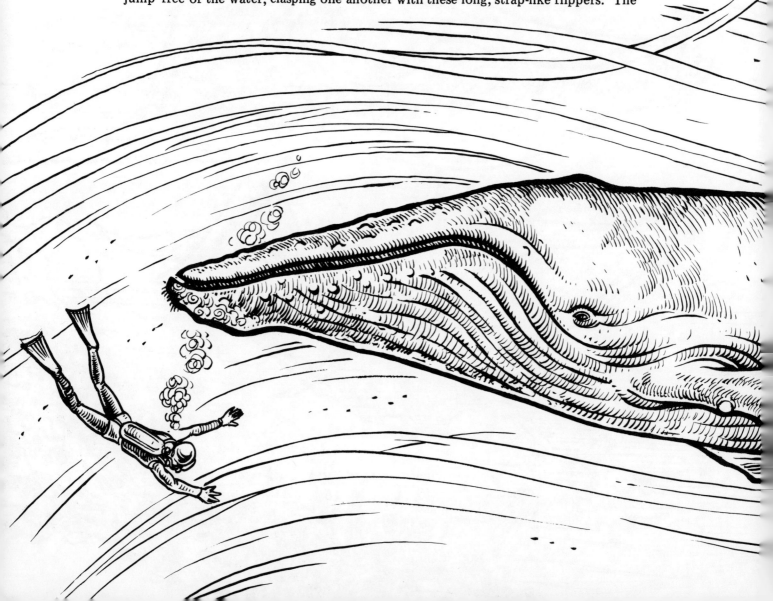

fins are often white, and may be seen for long distances underwater. Sometimes the flukes of the whales are splotched with white or are even completely white, and individual whales can be recognized by the patterns of their flukes, or by the shape of their peculiar fins. Humpback whales are not attractive by our standards since their heads are covered with lumps, and if one looks at these lumps one can see that each bears a long hair, remnants of the days when whales were fur-bearing animals, many millions of years ago. Like other whales, humpbacks carry inside of their bodies other evidences of past terrestrial animal ancestry. These are such things as the tiny remains of hind limb bones which can be found buried inside the bodies of whales, or the finger bones which lie inside their flippers. If one looks carefully, one can also see tiny ear openings on either side of the head of whales, which are likewise remnants of a time when these animals lived on land.

Black except for variable white on underside of flippers, belly, and occasionally on flukes.

Baird's Beaked Whale *(Berardius bairdi)*

Light gray, slightly lighter on the belly.

The largest of the beaked whales is Baird's beaked whale, which lives in the waters of the north Pacific. Beaked whales dwell mostly far out in the open sea and dive deeply into the ocean to catch their squid prey. Baird's beaked whales are probably relatives of the giant sperm whale, and like the sperm whale, have a spermaceti organ in their foreheads. Unlike most whales, they usually do not have a notch in the tail flukes, but instead have a straight fluke that extends from tip to tip without any indentation in it. Most of the beaked whales have tiny little dorsal fins, often set very far back on the body. Occasionally beaked whales can be seen leaping high out of the water, far off in the distance, and they seldom allow vessels to get very close to them, being quite shy. Because of their shyness the beaked whales are very seldom seen, so very little is actually known about most of them.

Some of the beaked whales have large teeth that stick out of the lower jaw; these teeth are very peculiar, flattened pieces of ivory that some people think serve to keep the two jaws lined up when the animal catches very large and strong squids. Baird's beaked whale has teeth that stick out of the tip of the lower jaw, and has a few more teeth back in the jaw. One of the beaked whales, the straptooth whale, has peculiar teeth that extend out of the lower jaw like ivory straps over the upper and actually prevent the animal from opening its jaws very wide. No one knows exactly how these teeth are used.

Beluga *(Delphinapterus leucas)*

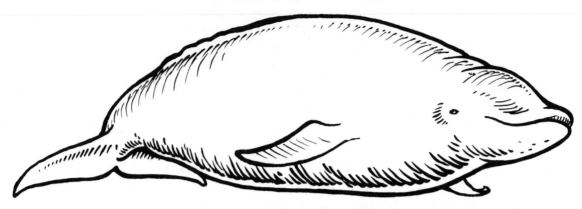

The beluga, or sea canary, lives in the cold waters of the northern hemisphere. It is often found in cracks, or leads, in the ice of the Arctic Ocean, and sometimes comes as far south as England or the northern United States. It has been called the sea canary because of the remarkable array of sounds it produces, including clicks, whistles, chirps, and a variety of other kinds of sounds. Baby belugas are born gray colored, and only become white when they are adults. Adult belugas are pure white: some people think that this is because they live amongst the ice cakes of the Arctic. Belugas have been hunted for the remarkable leather that can be made from their skins, which has been used to make fine gloves.

Belugas travel in very large groups, sometimes hundreds of animals gathering together in a single area. There are different populations of belugas around the world that can be told from one another by their different size. The beluga is known to swim long distances up rivers in search of its young salmon prey; it navigates across the muddy waters of the entrances to these rivers and is able to find its way among the mazes of channels with amazing facility. Belugas sometimes stay in icy areas and may keep areas of water open by their swimming movements: this allows them to breathe when the rest of the ocean surface is frozen. This habit makes them especially vulnerable to Eskimo hunters, for whom the beluga has long been an important food source, and many are captured when they exhibit this behavior.

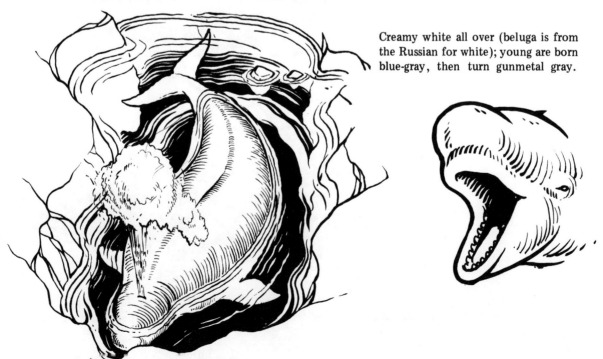

Creamy white all over (beluga is from the Russian for white); young are born blue-gray, then turn gunmetal gray.

Bowhead Whale *(Balaena mysticetus)* & Steam Whaleship

Here are two bowhead whales, a mother and her young, swimming amongst the ice of the Arctic. This species of whale was driven almost to extinction by the early whalers of the 1600s. The whalers first sought them in the oceans near Spitzbergen, anchoring their vessels in the coves and simply waiting for the whales to swim in. When they were caught they were rendered down for their rich oil, and the great quantities of baleen from this whale were taken. Baleen comes from the plates in the mouth of the whale, which form a strainer by means of which the whale captures the small swimming crustaceans that form its food. In the bowhead whale, the baleen is extremely long and flexible, and was once very valuable. This was before the age of plastics; this baleen was used for many of the same purposes as modern plastics. The bowhead whale is the only large whale that stays in the Arctic through-

Blackish (not as shiny as the right whale); most have a white patch under the chin and another white patch near the genitalia on the belly. The demarcation of colors is sharp.

out the year, staying near the ice edge even in the dark of the arctic night. Bowhead whales are now extremely rare, occurring only in the arctic waters of the Pacific Ocean, where perhaps 2,000 of the animals now live. They are protected except for a few which the Eskimos are allowed to take. The Eskimos have been fishing this whale for thousands of years. Its capture is involved with the coming of age of a young man and is extremely important to their society. The whales are divided up by the Eskimos once they are towed laboriously onto the ice. The captors get the largest portion but the rest of the village shares in the catch, too; the pieces of the whale are stored in pits in the frozen ground of the Eskimo village. With the protection now being afforded the bowhead whale, we hope that its numbers may increase and that it may once again become common in the Arctic waters of the world.

Sei Whales *(Balaenoptera borealis)*

These are Sei whales, which are medium-sized whales that have only recently been captured in large numbers by whalers. Before these modern times, Sei whales were either too swift for the whalers, as was the case when sailing vessels were used, or they produced too little oil to be of much value for the whaling industry. Now, however, they are being captured both for food, obtained from their meat, and for the small store of oil that they produce. Like other rorqual whales, they are swift-moving and undergo long migrations from the polar feeding grounds to calving

The belly is whitish up to the throat; a diffuse darkish band crosses the chest between the flippers. The upper surface is very dark gray; its white mottling is usually rather diffuse, but can be very sharp where lamprey eels have left 2 x 3" oblong scars.

grounds closer to the equator. One usually thinks of whales as being fat animals, but indeed the largest are really very slim. Apparently this is because these huge creatures have trouble losing the heat produced by their swimming movements and it is more efficient to lose heat if one is slim than if one is fat. The blubber of whales seems to be mostly a reserve of food, rather than a protective layer to keep the animal warm, since their very large bodies are, themselves, effective in storing heat.

Killer Whale *(Orcinus orca)* and Gray Seal *(Halichoerus grypus)*

Shiny black except for oblong white area, belly, eye, curves around flanks by back of fin; behind the dorsal fin there is a saddle of light gray which looks white when in the water.

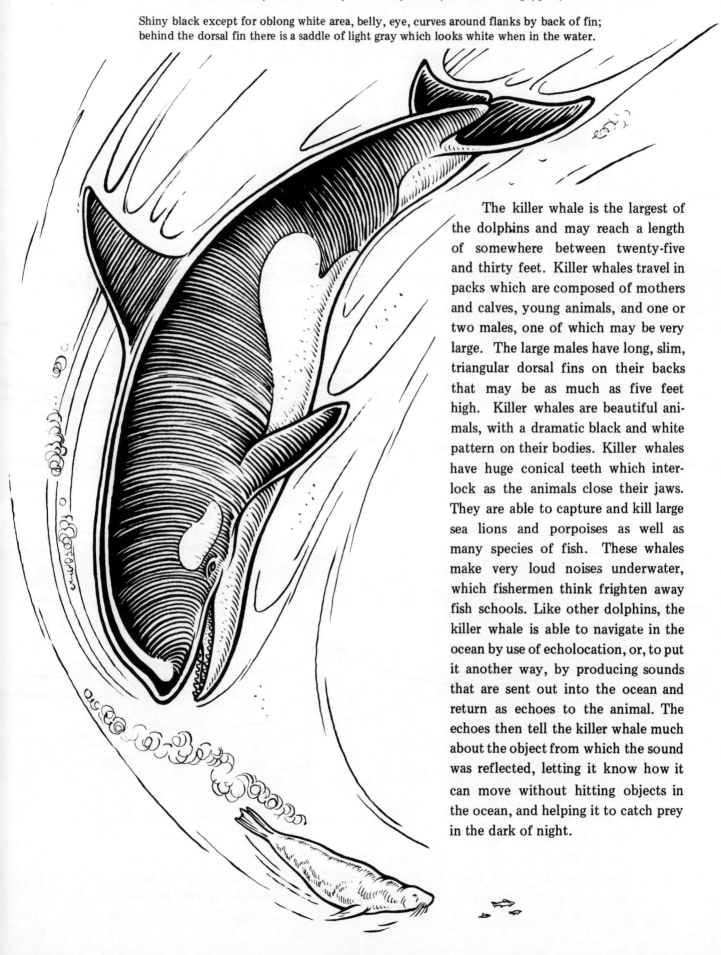

The killer whale is the largest of the dolphins and may reach a length of somewhere between twenty-five and thirty feet. Killer whales travel in packs which are composed of mothers and calves, young animals, and one or two males, one of which may be very large. The large males have long, slim, triangular dorsal fins on their backs that may be as much as five feet high. Killer whales are beautiful animals, with a dramatic black and white pattern on their bodies. Killer whales have huge conical teeth which interlock as the animals close their jaws. They are able to capture and kill large sea lions and porpoises as well as many species of fish. These whales make very loud noises underwater, which fishermen think frighten away fish schools. Like other dolphins, the killer whale is able to navigate in the ocean by use of echolocation, or, to put it another way, by producing sounds that are sent out into the ocean and return as echoes to the animal. The echoes then tell the killer whale much about the object from which the sound was reflected, letting it know how it can move without hitting objects in the ocean, and helping it to catch prey in the dark of night.

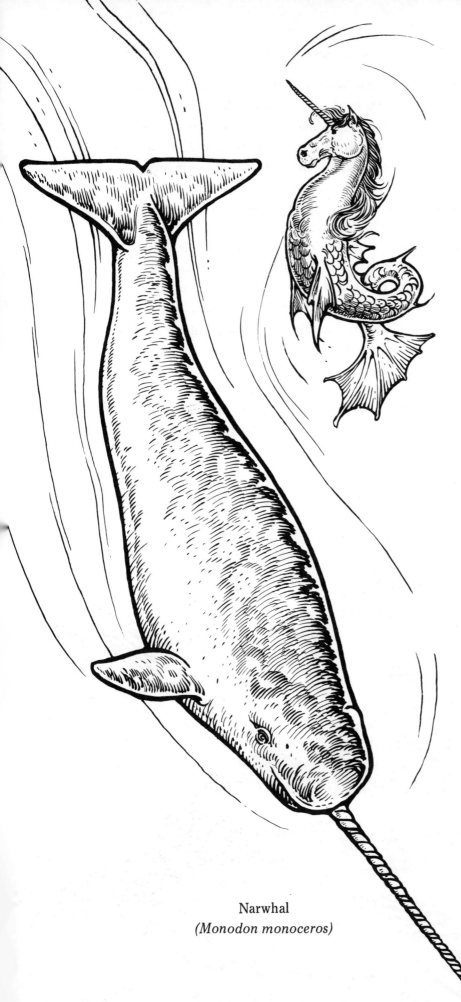

The narwhal is a peculiar animal that lives only near the ice edge up in the Arctic Ocean. It is a favorite food of some groups of Eskimos, who sometimes catch them in the winter when the narwhals, like the belugas, are keeping openings free of ice so that they can breathe. They are easy prey for an Eskimo with a kayak and a harpoon.

For several hundred years Europeans did not know what a narwhal was; they knew it only from the long twisted tusks brought back by explorers, sometimes seven or eight feet in length. Some people said this tusk projected from the forehead of a horse-like animal called the unicorn. But finally one explorer found a narwhal frozen in the ice with its tusk intact. It thus became clear that the tusks belonged to an ocean mammal, and not to a land-dwelling horse-like creature. But mystery continued to surround the narwhal, and its tusk was thought to have magical properties; in particular, it was thought to protect against poisons, and so kings and queens paid enormous sums for the tusks and had goblets made from which to drink their wine.

No one is really sure how narwhals use their tusks, though the tusks of males are longer than those of females. Sometimes narwhals are found with two tusks; the tusks are actually teeth which have been directed forward through the gum of the narwhal's mouth. The twisting of the tusk probably gives it the necessary strength to be so long and at the same time so thin.

Narwhal
(*Monodon monoceros*)

When molted, light gray on blue-gray background; looks almost speckled underwater.

White-sided Dolphin *(Lagenorhynchus acutus)*

Here we see the white-sided dolphin of the North Atlantic Ocean. This is one of the many species of schooling dolphins that live in the oceans of the world, both in the cool waters near the poles and in the warm waters near the equator. The schools that these animals form are their societies, and it is in them that all of the life of the animal takes place. They are born there, in a school that keeps swimming throughout its entire life, and they learn there to ride on their mother's side, carried along by her; they learn to nurse from their mother. She provides them with a rich milk which lets them grow very rapidly. It is in these schools that they dive into the ocean to catch their prey, which consists mostly of fish and squid, and it is in these schools that they find their protection from predators. These predators are such animals as the great sharks, that may swim up from below and attempt to catch unwary stragglers. The school itself helps to protect the dolphins by providing a great many alert animals to listen and look in all directions as the school moves along and warn all the other school members should a predator appear. Dolphins swim fairly rapidly in the ocean, though not so rapidly as most people think. Most of the dolphins, like the white-sided dolphin, seldom swim more than eight or ten knots, though they can reach speeds of fifteen to twenty knots for very brief periods. Many fishes can swim much faster than dolphins can. The marlin and the swordfish can apparently swim as fast as fifty knots.

Light gray or whitish, with "suspender" stripes over shoulders and neck; there are distinct streaks of a bit of brown tinge on the sides.

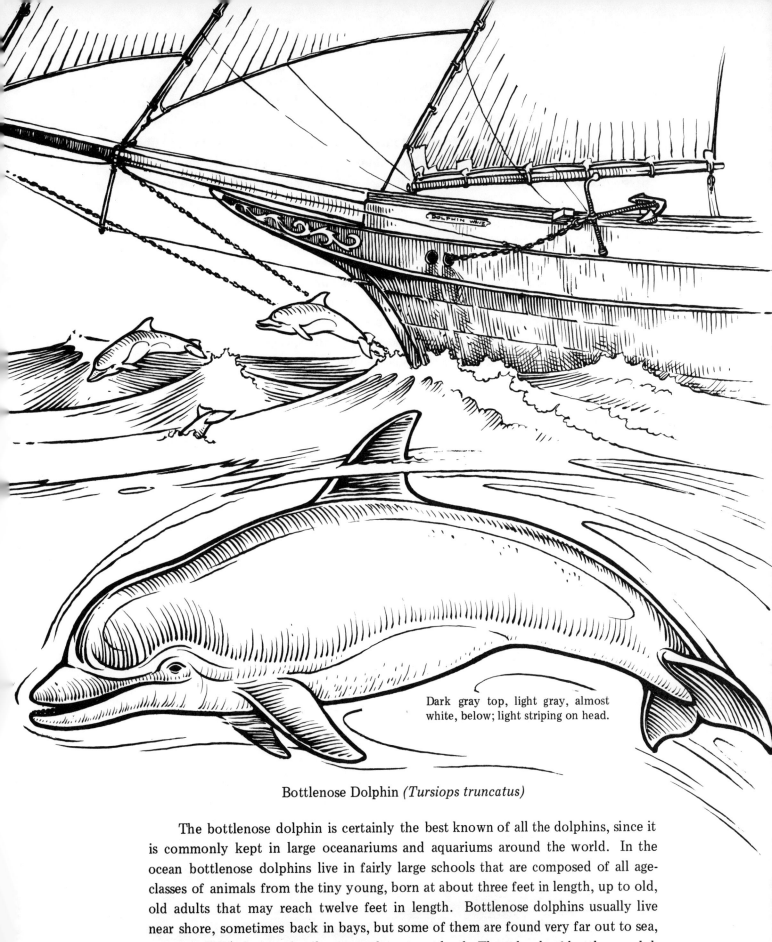

Dark gray top, light gray, almost white, below; light striping on head.

Bottlenose Dolphin *(Tursiops truncatus)*

The bottlenose dolphin is certainly the best known of all the dolphins, since it is commonly kept in large oceanariums and aquariums around the world. In the ocean bottlenose dolphins live in fairly large schools that are composed of all age-classes of animals from the tiny young, born at about three feet in length, up to old, old adults that may reach twelve feet in length. Bottlenose dolphins usually live near shore, sometimes back in bays, but some of them are found very far out to sea, occasionally a thousand miles from the nearest land. The schools of bottlenose dolphins are their societies, and when a young bottlenose dolphin is born the mother may be accompanied by another dolphin, usually a female, called an "auntie porpoise," that may help the young one to the surface. Adult male bottlenose dolphins may chase the baby at birth, and it seems that in the ocean this serves to keep the mother and young in the center of the school, which is the safest place from shark attack. The calf may swim with the mother for many miles on the first day it is born by catching a free ride on her side; it presses its little flipper to her side, and the rushing water passing between baby and mother sucks it in close to her side and it is able to simply be carried along without moving a muscle. The baby gets this kind of free ride for the first few months of its life until it is completely on its own. The little calf grows rapidly, and nurses from its mother many times a day. It slides down her tail and forces its beak into one of two slits on the tail where the mammary glands are located. The milk is very much richer than cow's milk and causes the baby to put on a good blubber coat to keep it warm in the ocean. Juvenile bottlenose porpoises often gather in groups that will gambol about in the middle of the whole dolphin school. When the young dolphin finally becomes an adult, it takes its place as either a guardian of the school, or gives birth to new calves.

Bottlenose dolphins like to eat a lot of different kinds of sea food, including fishes, and squids, and sometimes things like crabs that they pick up off the sea bottom. Bottlenose dolphins are also very curious, and learn very rapidly. They may learn, for example, that a shrimp boat will shovel waste fish over its rail after the net has been brought in, and that this waste may contain a lot of small fish; bottlenose dolphins may swim for miles to reach one of these boats when they hear the net coming aboard. They learn other things, too, about the world they live in, such as places where the tide might trap them, or where they can get across a narrow channel, or where they can find foods of different sorts. Sometimes they catch flying fish by swimming along rapidly underwater as the flying fish skims in the air, capturing it when it falls back into the sea.

Bottlenose dolphins have proven to be very intelligent, and in captivity they learn a great many tricks very rapidly. They are also remarkably friendly animals that are very hardy compared to many other marine mammals. Bottlenose dolphins can hear sounds that are as much as ten times as high as a human can hear, and they can make sounds higher than we can hear, too. No one really knows how they use their whistles, groans, barks and other noises, except that they are somehow used socially, and that some of them are used to find food. But no one can yet be sure whether or not they have anything like a language.

Profiles of bottlenose whales on surface.
See next page

Bottlenosed Whale *(Hyperoodon ampullatus)*

BOTTLENOSE WHALE. Fully developed male (top) and female.
Development of "Flathead" in male below, right to left.

Gray P. 25
London 1883

The bottlenose whale is another member of the beaked whale family, and it occurs in both the southern and northern hemispheres of the ocean. It has been fished for a long time by whalers because of the valuable oil found in the case inside the smooth surface of the animal's head. Bottlenose whales are curious animals, and the old whalers knew that if they stopped their boat in certain places in the ocean the bottlenose whales would simply swim up to them out of curiosity and then they could be caught. One such place where bottlenose whales come is called the Gully, off the coast of Novia Scotia in the Atlantic Ocean: a few of these now rare whales can sometimes be found there.

Dark color, with the belly a bit lighter; there are
scratches on the body as though hit by a board.

Risso's Dolphin *(Grampus griseus)*

Here we see the grampus, or Risso's dolphin. This big, swift, ponderous dolphin
lives all over the world's oceans. When one sees an old Risso's dolphin it is almost
always scarred with the marks of squid tentacles, especially around its mouth, where
the thrashing squid have scratched deep into its skin on many, many encounters.
Risso's dolphins have been captured a few times and kept in the big oceanic aquariums, or oceanaria, and there they have proven to be easily trainable. They perform high leaps from the water to take food from a trainer's hands. Risso's dolphin feeds almost entirely upon squid, and like many squid-feeders has very rough
gums for holding the squid instead of the numerous teeth that other dolphins have.

Common Dolphin
(Delphinus delphus)

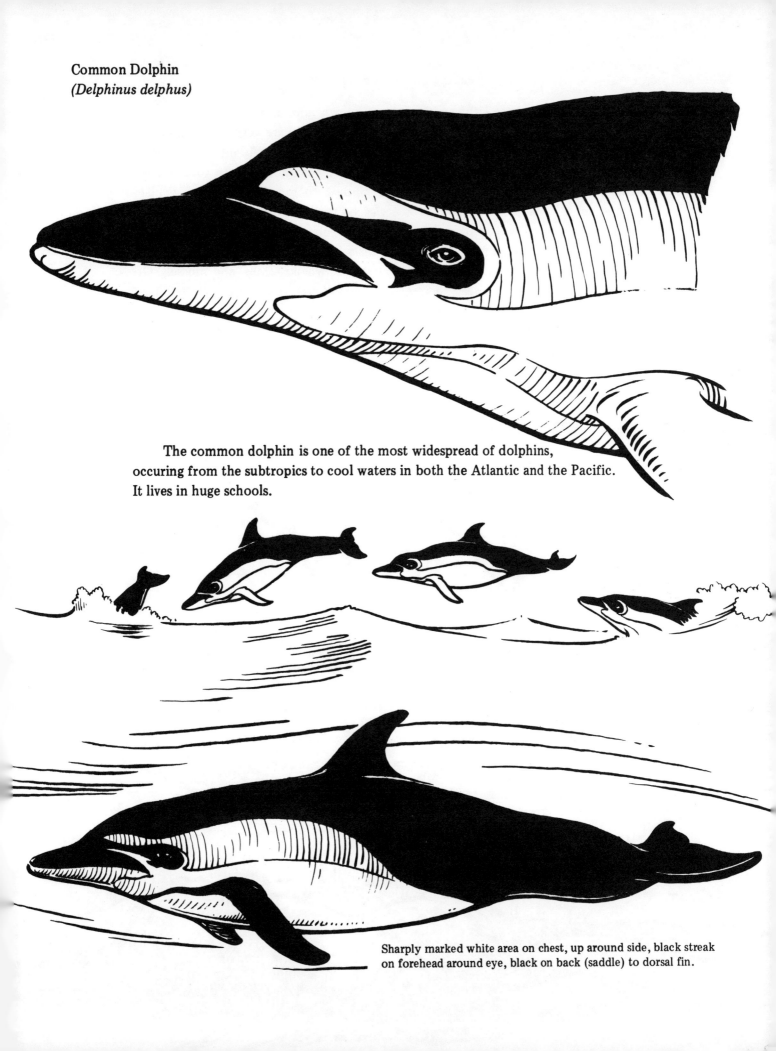

The common dolphin is one of the most widespread of dolphins, occuring from the subtropics to cool waters in both the Atlantic and the Pacific. It lives in huge schools.

Sharply marked white area on chest, up around side, black streak on forehead around eye, black on back (saddle) to dorsal fin.

Harbor Seal (*Phoca vitulina*)

Harbor seals, *Phoca vitulina*, are so well known in so many areas of the world that they are frequently called "common" seals, yet they are very shy animals and difficult to approach. Harbor seals are found in both the Atlantic and Pacific Oceans, in temperate waters. These animals usually do not migrate to any great extent; small populations of harbor seals appear to remain in the same place throughout the year. Usually seen in estuaries, on sand banks uncovered at low tide, and near river mouths, harbor seals are easily recognized by the many dark spots on their gray fur. Fish is the main diet of these seals, although off the British coast they are known to sample eel, and they also eat squids, whelks, crabs, and mussels. Off the California coast, harbor seals themselves often fall prey to the Great White Shark.

There is a great variation in color and pattern of spots, but generally they are a light gray with irregular spots of black, and lighter on the underside.

Bearded Seal (*Erignathus barbatus*)

The bearded seal, *Erignathus barbatus*, lives all around the North Pole, with some populations found in Europe, Asia, and North America, as well as in the Arctic Ocean. It is a shy animal and therefore not very well known, and is never found in very large numbers. It is thought that there are from 75,000 to 150,000 bearded seals in the world. Both the male and the female are about the same size, weighing from 500 to 600 pounds, and reaching a length of about seven and a half feet. The pups are born on ice floes in April and May, where the bearded seal's enemies, Eskimos and polar bears, live.

Like the walrus, the bearded seal has a remarkable profusion of long whiskers. Also like the walrus, it feeds on the sea bottom on shrimp, crabs, clams, whelks, snails, octopuses, and bottom fish like sculpin. At certain times of the year their livers contain so much Vitamin A that bearded seals become poisonous, and even sled dogs in the arctic have learned not to eat them.

Gray with a slightly brown or reddish tinge on the head

California Sea Lion *(Zalophus californianus)*

The California sea lion, *Zalophus californianus*, is one of the best known of pinnipeds, being found in zoos around the world. The female of the species is also the most frequent performer in trained seal acts in circuses. The male is larger by one foot than the female, who is six feet in length, but he outweighs her by several hundred pounds: she weighs only 200 pounds to his 600 to 800 pounds. The male can also be distinguished from the female by the bump on his head, the dorsal crest.

California sea lions feed on squid, octopus, herring, rockfish, hake and other fishes. These animals live along coastal areas, and are rarely seen farther out to sea than about fifteen miles. They breed along the coast of California, in the Gulf of California, off Baja California and Mexico, and in and around the Galapagos Islands, as well as off the Japanese coast. The largest breeding areas, or rookeries, are in southern California, on San Nicolas island, and San Miguel Island. Sea lions breed in summer. Adult males defend the territories where the females come to give birth against each other, and it is here that breeding also takes place.

Chocolate brown, the females somewhat lighter than the males. There is a considerable variation in color from wet to dry state: females are tawny or buff when dry. The sagittal crest of the adult male gets lighter with age.

Elephant Seal *(Mirounga angustirostris)*

It is not difficult to see where the elephant seal, *Mirounga angustirostris*, gets its name. The adult male has a long elephantine-looking nose, which is a secondary sex characteristic; when a male becomes sexually mature, the nose starts to grow, just as the antlers on a stag began to appear as the stag becomes an adult. It is also a sign to other males that the one with the big nose is an adult. If two males meet in the water, very often one will simply lift his nose out of the water and show it to the other male, who thereupon turns around and flees.

Elephant seals feed deep in the water, at 600 feet or below, typically eating shark, skate, ratfish, and squid. Northern elephant seals, who live off the coast of California and Mexico, breed during the winter months. The males fight with each other for status in a pecking order, for only the few males at the very top of this order, the best fighters, do all the mating with the females. When the pups are born they weigh about eighty pounds; by the time they are weaned from mother's milk, only four weeks old, they weigh between 280 to 300 pounds. The mother elephant seal is unusual for a mammal, for she does not feed while she is nursing her baby: all of the food comes from her own body stores.

The elephant seal population was reduced by sealers in the 1880s to less than a hundred. Fortunately, they have made a fantastic recovery, and today there are about 60,000 in existence.

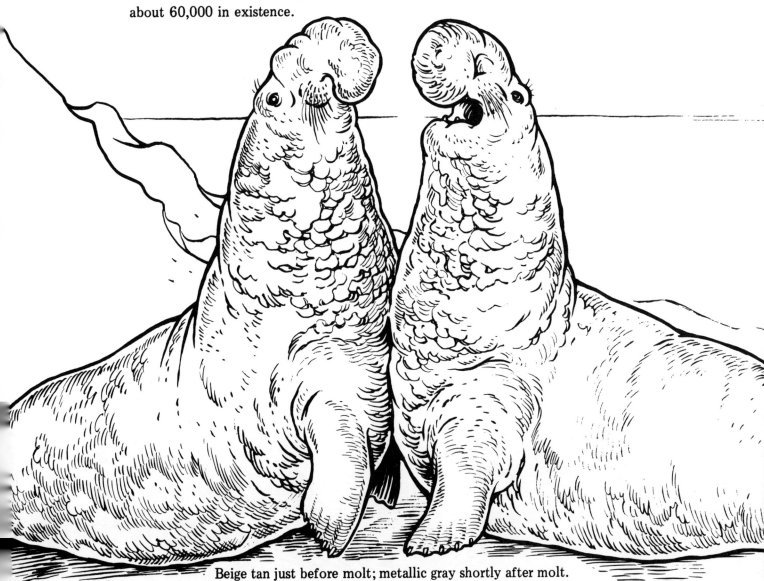

Beige tan just before molt; metallic gray shortly after molt.

Northern Fur Seal *(Callorhinus ursinus)*

The northern fur seal, *Callorhinus ursinus*, is one of the most sociable of all the pinnipeds. About one and a half million of these animals breed during the winter on two tiny islands in the Bering Sea, the Pribilof Islands, as well as on a few other islands off the Siberian coast, and, strangely enough, on one island off the coast of southern California, San Miguel Island. Mating takes place within each male's particular territory, which he obstinately defends against all other males. There, a male may mate with fifty to one hundred different females. During the winter months, the fur seals migrate south in order to feed, with the females usually migrating farther than do the males. They travel long distances down the west coast of North America, often as far south as San Diego, and down to the coast of Japan on the other side of the Pacific. Each year they return to the breeding area of the previous year, and the entire process is repeated.

The fur on these animals is very rich and fine and keeps the seals perfectly dry, for water cannot penetrate the fur and touch their skin. The beautiful fur of the northern fur seal is also a much desired item on the fashion market; in order to limit the number of skins taken each year to protect the population of the fur seal, a treaty was signed in 1912 by the four major exploiters of the fur: the United States, Canada, Japan and the U.S.S.R. Each year about 50,000 skins are taken from the Pribilofs, processed in the United States and then sold on the open market, with the proceeds divided amongst the four countries.

Males: dark rich brown with slightly gray shoulders
Females: dark gray back, light gray underside of neck and chest

Walrus *(Odobenus rosmarus)*

The earliest known fossil of the walrus, *Odobenus rosmarus*, is about fifteen million years old. Yet, after all this time, very little is known about these creatures who are recognized the world over, or about their social and reproductive behavior. They live in the shallow waters surrounding the arctic coasts around the North Pole, and breed during the winter in places very difficult to be reached by scientists who wish to study their behavior. Recently, however, some investigators have been able to put tiny radio transmitters on the tusks of some walruses in order to follow their daily movements over a long period of time, in the hope of finding out more about these odd-looking creatures.

Both male and female walruses have the long tusks which are their most noticeable feature, although those of the female are more slender. Walruses are very large animals; an adult male reaches a length of twelve feet, and can weigh up to 2000 pounds, while the female is only slightly smaller. Walruses feed primarily in shallow water on several species of clams, although the remains of young seals and even young walruses have been found in their stomachs.

The young have a thin coat of reddish brown hair; the skin is nearly smooth on old animals.

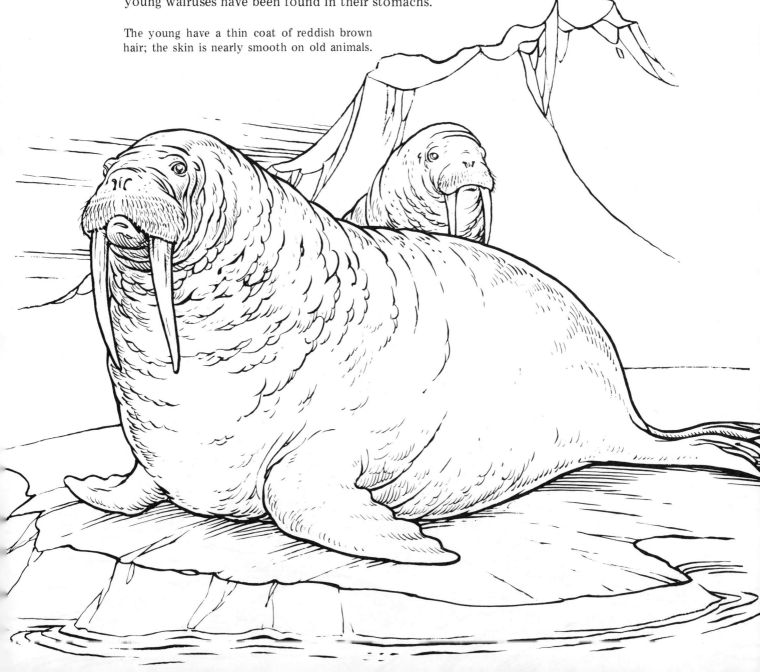

The Sea Otter
(*Enhydra lutris*)

The story of the sea otter is a long one, and at one time it was almost a disastrous one. It is the story of a river and lake species from Asia adapting to almost five million years of life in the ocean, adjusting to predation by aboriginal hunters for perhaps tens of thousands of years, facing near extinction at the hands of the fur traders, and, under protection, now slowly returning to portions of its former range.

The sea otter is a member of the family *Mustelidae* which includes the skunks, weasels, badger, marten, wolverine, fisher, mink, and, the closest cousins to the sea otters, the river otters. The sea otter is one of the largest of the mustelids, exceeded in size only by the giant river otter of South America. It differs from other members of this family in its total adaptation to a marine existence, including giving birth to young while floating in water, and in its loss of the anal scent glands that make some members of this family poor company.

Brownish fur when born, with yellowish guard hair and a light buff head. An adult has a dark brown body with the head varying in color from brown to white.

Of all the sea mammals including the whales, porpoises, seals, sea lions, walrus, and manatees, the sea otter is the only species that did not develop a thick layer of blubber under the skin for thermo-insulation. When the ancient ancestor of the sea otter, *Enhydriodon*, entered the ocean from the rivers and lakes of Asia during the border between the Miocene and Pliocene periods some 4.5 to 5 million years ago, there must have been a rich supply of food available to this efficient species throughout the north Pacific coastlines. However, the food that could be eaten by this new marine species was already pre-determined by the type of teeth *Enhydriodon* possessed which were those of a "crabeater." These teeth included large rounded molars for crushing and stout blunt canines for prying. Even though the ocean abounds with many species of fishes, unlike most of the other marine mammals, the sea otter could not take advantage of this source of energy. Its teeth were not adapted to capture fish under water, and, if it was like the present species, it could not swim rapidly enough under the water for more than five minutes. Therefore, shellfish including crabs, clams, urchins, abalones, snails, barnacles, and octopuses became the principal diet. There are a few very sluggish fish species in cold Alaskan waters that the otter can catch with its forepaws and bring to the surface to kill and eat, but these fishes are not abundant enough in Alaska to furnish a steady diet and are either not present or rare south of Alaska.

Enhydriodon evolved into two species, *Enhydra macrodonta* and *Enhydra lutris* with only *E. lutris* surviving. At the beginning of the fur trade period in 1741, this species ranged from northern Japan north along the Kurile Islands and Kamchatka Peninsula, throughout the Commander, Aleutian, and Pribilof Islands, along the southern coastline of Alaska and south along the Pacific coast into southern Baja California, a shoreline distance of over 6,000 miles. The limit to distribution to the north was the formation of winter sea ice, and either lack of food or constant high temperature limited the southern distribution. Unlike the river otter, which can maneuver agilely on land, the sea otter developed highly specialized hind flippers, whose fifth digit (in other animals the outside "little" finger) is the longest. This specialized flipper, for water locomotion, prevented the sea otter from leaving the water's edge for more than a few meters because its clumsiness on land made it difficult to escape large predators. Thus, the sea otter became restricted to a total marine life, eating primarily shellfish.

Since the sea otter has no blubber for insulation, its body temperature of 38.1°C (about 100°F) must be maintained by the insulation of its thick, dense fur and by a high metabolic rate. Grooming bouts are undertaken after each feeding period to keep food particles out of the fur. The mother also grooms her pup for long periods, using her tongue and paws to manipulate the fur. Air particles are trapped between the tiny hairs, forming a cushion of air that prevents any water from reaching the skin. The sea otter's fur is one of the thickest and densest of all mammal furs and is considered to be highest in quality. It varies in shades of brown. There are around 800 million hairs on a large adult. Each guard hair is surrounded by from sixty to eighty underfur hairs forming a bundle emerging through a common skin pore. The guard hairs on a newly born pup are longer than in the adult and are usually light brown to yellowish. These long hairs resulted in the term "wooly pup" given to pups up to about two months of age. Even though this fur is one of the densest of all mammal furs, considerable heat is still lost to the water through the fur. Experiments have shown that about sixty percent of the body heat is lost through the appendages where the fur is quite thin. Consequently, the sea otter has learned to keep its paws and flippers out of the water as much as possible when resting and grooming.

If an otter is only slightly disturbed while resting on its back with its paws, flippers, and, usually, tail extended into the air, the animal will attempt to slowly move about while remaining on its back with its appendages out of the water. The otter may even turn around several times from its back to its belly while at the same time keeping its paws and flippers out of the water. Only when greatly disturbed will a resting animal dive and get its appendages wet. On the other hand, wetting the paws and flippers can be used to cool off the body temperature if the animal becomes too warm. The fur's condition is so important to the otter that it spends much of its daily activity in grooming. Part of the grooming process is to replace the tiny air bubbles that have been lost while diving. The animal does this by turning summersaults in the water and blowing bubbles under itself, then patting these bubbles into the fur with its forepaws.

We have seen that the fur is important to retain body heat, but considerable heat is still lost through the fur. Therefore the principal factor in keeping the high temperature and other body functions going is a high metabolic rate, some 2.5 times the average for mammals. Sea otters must eat two to five times per day and take in food equal to twenty-five percent of their weight daily. This amounts to about 5,000 to 8,000 calories per day, which is about three times what an adult human must consume in a day. Food travels through the gastro-intestinal tract within three hours, so it is necessary for otters to eat several times a day, and also at night. Otters can capture their prey in the dark by locating it with their sensitive forepaws. A loose paunch of skin under each foreleg may be used to temporarily store and transport food until it can be consumed at the water's surface. Sea otters are opportunistic feeders, selecting from over forty different marine animals found on the ocean bottom and in kelp (giant seaweed) beds. These items include sea urchins, mussels, clams, abalones, crabs, and snails. While most of the prey otters favor is not taken by man, some commercial and recreational shellfishing may not be possible in the sea otter's range. Since otters are the chief harvesters of sea urchins, and since urchins feed on the root-like structures of kelp, removal of the urchins by the sea otters increases the size of the kelp beds, thus increasing food and cover for other marine life which depends on the kelp habitat.

What limits the sea otter population?

If the otter does not eat it will lose 10 percent of its weight each day, and in three days without food it may die. Sea otter researchers in Russia, Alaska, and

California have come to the conclusion that ultimately food is a limiting factor. Sea otters who have difficulty foraging during the harsh winter months may starve. The sea otter has no diseases that can cause death, and even though they have internal parasites, these injurious worms are not a primary cause of mortality. The otter has no external parasites. The otter also does not have any natural predators that can limit its numbers. White sharks are known to attack sea otters in California and Oregon, and in Alaska bald eagles prey upon small pups floating on the surface while the mother is below searching for food. Killer whales are not predators, although one possible attack of a killer whale on an otter was noted in the Kuriles many years ago.

Its Life History

We have seen that the otter consumes lots of food each day to stay alive and consequently most of its behavior is designed to secure food items and conserve heat. Otters have been known to dive to a depth of 97 meters (318 feet), but since most of their food is rarely found deeper than 30 meters (98 feet), few dives are deeper than this. Females can have a pup every year; the mother cares for the offspring for from five to eight months. A mother nurses her pup with her milk during its first few months, and by four months the pup is eating solid food obtained by its

mother. A pup will weigh from 2½ to 3½ pounds when born and within a year may weigh up to 20 to 25 pounds. The largest adult otter taken in Alaska weighed 102 pounds, the largest in California 92 pounds. In general, California sea otters are smaller than those in Alaska; the females average 46 pounds and the males 56 pounds. A behavior unique to the otter is the use of tools to gather and break hard-shelled food items. The otter will use a rock or other hard object to remove shellfish such as abalones, mussels and barnacles, which are attached to a hard substrate. A rock is placed on the otter's chest, then clams and other hard food items are held in the forepaws and pounded against it until broken. Along clam beaches the otter will place one clam on its chest and pound another against it.

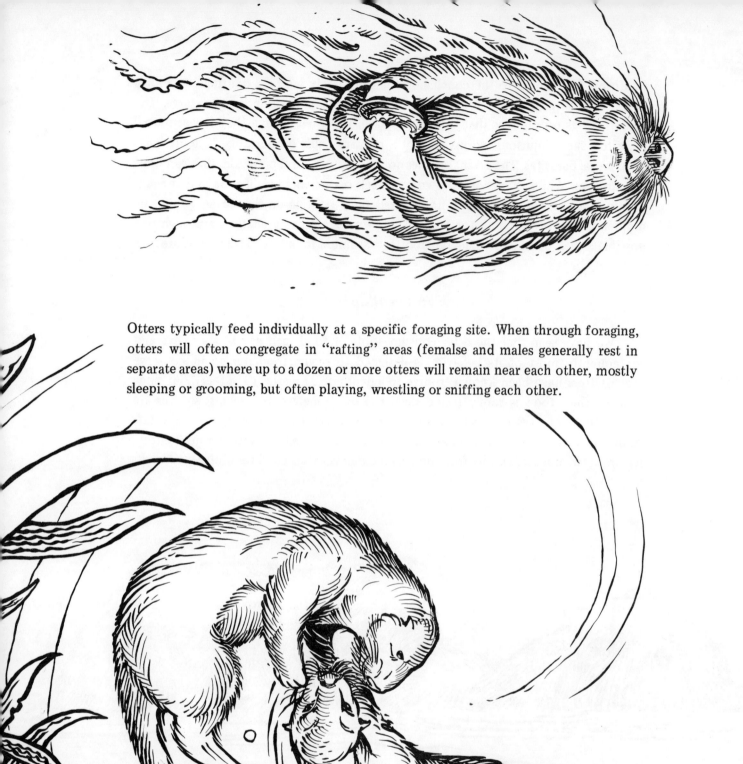

Otters typically feed individually at a specific foraging site. When through foraging, otters will often congregate in "rafting" areas (femalse and males generally rest in separate areas) where up to a dozen or more otters will remain near each other, mostly sleeping or grooming, but often playing, wrestling or sniffing each other.

The Presidio of Monterey   prior to 1822

The first encounter with man was probably when the first human migrants entered northern Japan and the mainland of Asia, but our knowledge of aboriginal hunting pressure comes from the evidence in Indian middens in the Aleutians and southward into California. Around three to four thousand years ago the Aleuts developed hunting methods which kept the otters at low levels, possibly at rare levels in some places. Other tribes throughout the range also hunted the otter for the furs which had high value to chieftans and for trading by coastal tribes. Nowhere, however, did aboriginal hunting seriously curtail the otter population as did the fur trade first initiated by the Russians in 1741. The otter fur trade actually opened up the northern Pacific coast to exploration and occupation. Soon after the Russian fur traders began working eastward through the Aleutians, Captain Cook discovered sea otters from what is now called British Columbia through the Aleutian Islands and alerted the western world of riches to be made. The Russians with their Aleut spear hunters eventually established their southernmost outpost at Fort Ross, California in 1812. Even though Spain and then Mexico attempted to keep otter hunters controlled and out of their waters, heavy hunting went on, ending with the appearance of American hunters in about 1830. Unlike the Russians' Aleut hunters, the Americans used guns, and within a very short period of about 30 years most of the otters were killed. In 1911 an international treaty was signed protecting the otters on the high seas. In 1913 laws were enacted in the Territory of Alaska and in the state of California to fully protect the sea otter. By 1926 the Russians stopped hunting them in the Kuriles. For most of the fur trade period nearly all the pelts were sent to China.

In 1913 there were only 50 to 100 otters left in California, near Point Sur. In Alaska from 1,000 to 2,000 otters remained in six isolated remnants. Under protection the population has built up to perhaps 150,000 in Alaska. Unfortunately, in California the sea otter has regained but a tenuous foothold. Today only an estimated 1,400 adult animals survive within a 220-mile long established range off the Central California coastal counties of Santa Cruz, Monterey and San Luis Obispo. The population is menaced by shootings, drowning in fishing nets, threats from shellfishermen and habitat pollution. Today the greatest threat to the otter is from a catastrophic oil spill. Should the otter's fur become matted with oil, allowing chilling ocean water to penetrate to the skin, death from exposure can come within hours. It is primarily because of this threat that the sea otter in California is listed as Threatened under the federal Endangered Species Act. Thus, if the sea otter is to survive into the twenty-first century, it will need our vigorous protection.

The Customs House, Monterey, prior to 1846